The Book of The Books

NO BOOK

OSHO

What you are holding in your hands is the compilation of all the gaps that Osho has deliberately left between his words. "I use words, so that you can fall deeper into the silent gaps," he says. The silent empty pages of this book are potent enough to guide us to our true nature – if we meditate upon them. And if we can't, Osho's words are there to help us, support us until we are finally able to grasp the gaps.

• Sharing Osho - Zorba Designs

• Hotel Surya Villa, Lane-A, Koregaon Park, Pune 411001. INDIA

• Tel. +91 9890347025, 20 26050859

• Email - zorbadesigns@gmail.com • info@zorbadesigns.com

• www.zorbadesigns.com • http://oshoheritage.org

• Exclusively reproduced limited number of copies for Osho centers, libraries, individual disciples and Osho lovers

Books have been written but God cannot be written. How will the books tell about Him? You wish to read the unwritten. Read the Vedas, the Gurugranth, the Koran; leave the written words and attend to the unwritten. Read the space between the lines, between the words, and remember what you have read.

If you read and concentrate on the written word you will become a pundit or a priest. If you read the unread, you become a sage. If you concentrate on the written word you will acquire a lot of information ; if you remember the unwritten, you will become like a child – innocent, artless.

Remember, the unwritten is the door.

Books have been written but God cannot be written. How will the books tell about Him? You wish to read the unwritten. Read the Vedas, the Gurugranth, the Koran; leave the written words and attend to the unwritten. Read the space between the lines, between the words, and remember what you have read.

If you read and concentrate on the written word you will become a pundit or a priest. If you read the unread, you become a sage. If you concentrate on the written word you will acquire a lot of information. If you remember the unwritten, you will become like a child – innocent, artless.

Remember, the unwritten is the door.

The ultimate will knock at your door only when you are not there. When you are absent, you are ready, because when you are absent only then is there a space for the ultimate to enter into you. Then you become a womb. If *you* are there you are always too much; there is not even a slight gap, space, for the ultimate to enter into you – and the ultimate is *vast*. You have to be so vastly empty, so infinitely empty – only then is there a possibility of the meeting.

The ultimate will knock at your door only when you are not there. When you are absent, you are ready, because when you are absent only then is there a space for the ultimate to enter into you. Then you become a womb. If *you* are there you are always too much; there is not even a slight gap, space, for the ultimate to enter into you – and the ultimate is *vast*. You have to be so vastly empty, so infinitely empty – only then is there a possibility of the meeting.

You have to forget, you have to unlearn all that you know. In the space of unlearning your innocence starts growing. I speak just to help you to understand my silent gaps. But what I am really doing is in the silences – not through the words, but between the words. Words are just toys that I am giving to your mind to play with. Silence is really the sword that penetrates directly into your heart; it brings transformation.

You have to forget, you have to unlearn all that you know. In the space of unlearning your innocence starts growing. I speak just to help you to understand my silent gaps. But what I am really doing is in the silences – not through the words, but between the words. Words are just toys that I am giving to your mind to play with. Silence is really the sword that penetrates directly into your heart; it brings transformation.

Silence is a difficult phenomenon, the most difficult to understand. It needs tremendous intelligence; not only intelligence, it needs a certain silence in you too. Then only, two silences can commune. And the world does not teach you to be silent; it teaches you words, language.

I have to use words and language so that you become caught in the net. Once you are caught and cannot escape, then you will have to listen to my silence too. And once you have understood my words, you will start feeling the silence that surrounds those words. Those words are born out of silence; they carry something of silence in them, some fragrance around them.

Silence is a difficult phenomenon, the most difficult to understand. It needs tremendous intelligence; not only intelligence, it needs a certain silence in you too. Then only, two silences can commune. And the world does not teach you to be silent; it teaches you words, language.

I have to use words and language so that you become caught in the net. Once you are caught and cannot escape, then you will have to listen to my silence too. And once you have understood my words, you will start feeling the silence that surrounds those words. Those words are born out of silence; they carry something of silence in them, some fragrance around them.

Catch the emptinesses, drink in the silences. Do not bother about what I am saying – I don't bother about what I am saying. I am not concerned today with what I said yesterday, and tomorrow I will not be concerned with what I am saying today. Yesterday I opened the door to my emptiness through certain words, today I am opening it through different words. For me, what is relevant is that emptiness which comes between the words...

Catch the emptinesses, drink in the silences. Do not bother about what I am saying – I don't bother about what I am saying. I am not concerned today with what I said yesterday, and tomorrow I will not be concerned with what I am saying today. Yesterday I opened the door to my emptiness through certain words, today I am opening it through different words. For me, what is relevant is that emptiness which comes between the words...

Once in a while, moving with me, flowing with me, hearing my words, listening to my silences, once in a while it happens. And those moments are of grace. In those moments you have the first taste of God. Slowly slowly, you will become more and more capable. That's why I go on speaking.

Once in a while, moving with me, flowing with me, hearing my words, listening to my silences, once in a while it happens. And those moments are of grace. In those moments you have the first taste of God. Slowly slowly, you will become more and more capable. That's why I go on speaking.

When you have heard a profound truth and the master becomes silent, suddenly words disappear and the presence of the master fills your heart. Something transpires in those silent moments, which nobody has ever been able to say, and nobody will ever be able to say. That transfer is possible only when the master is silent and the disciples are silent. Where two silences meet you experience the highest value; you experience love.

When you have heard a profound truth and the master becomes silent, suddenly words disappear and the presence of the master fills your heart. Something transpires in those silent moments, which nobody has ever been able to say, and nobody will ever be able to say. That transfer is possible only when the master is silent and the disciples are silent. Where two silences meet you experience the highest value; you experience love.

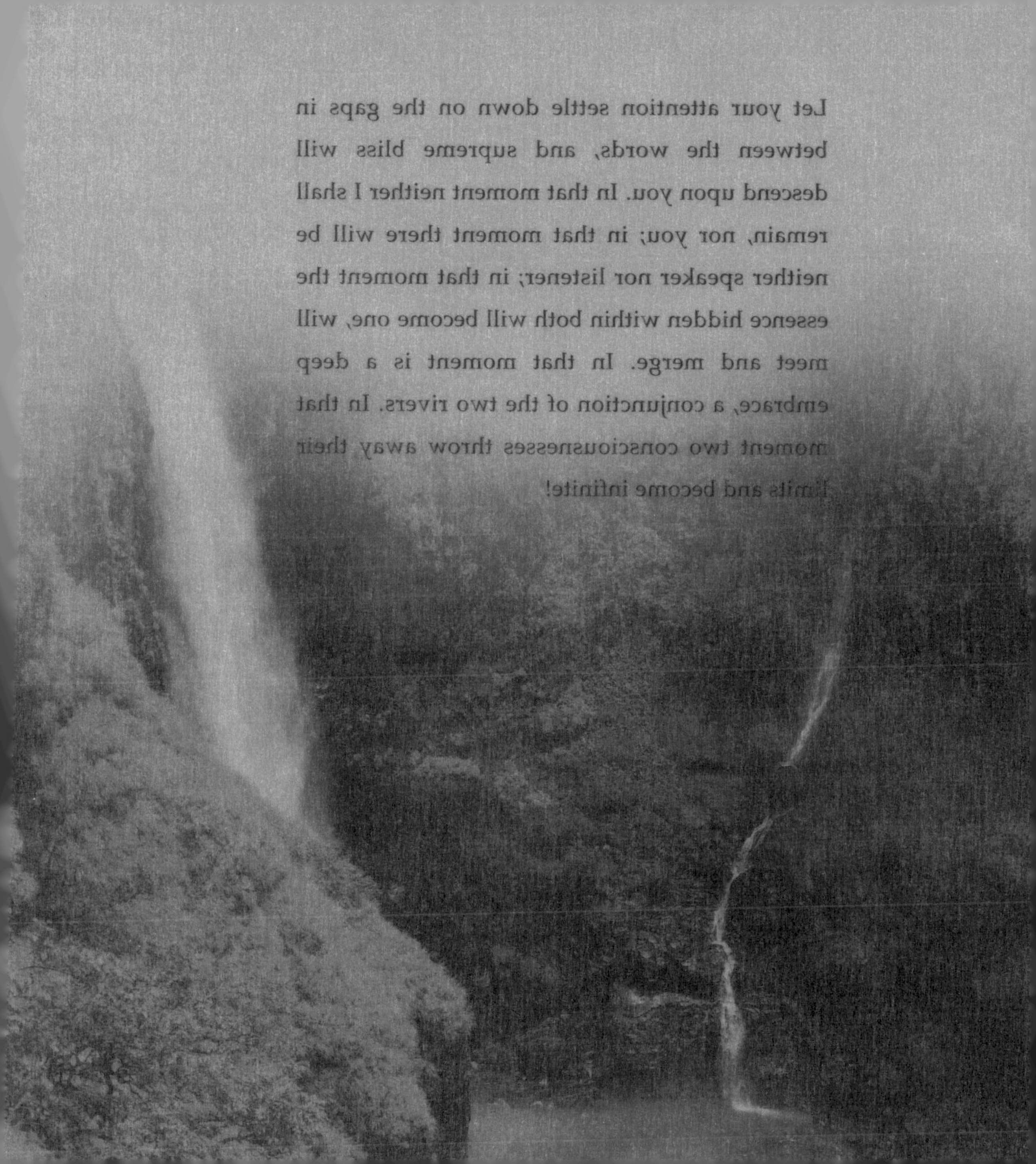

Let your attention settle down on the gaps in between the words, and supreme bliss will descend upon you. In that moment neither I shall remain, nor you; in that moment there will be neither speaker nor listener; in that moment the essence hidden within both will become one, will meet and merge. In that moment is a deep embrace, a conjunction of the two rivers. In that moment two consciousnesses throw away their limits and become infinite!

Let your attention settle down on the gaps in between the words, and supreme bliss will descend upon you. In that moment neither I shall remain, nor you; in that moment there will be neither speaker nor listener; in that moment the essence hidden within both will become one, will meet and merge. In that moment is a deep embrace, a conjunction of the two rivers. In that moment two consciousnesses throw away their limits and become infinite!

Emptiness can never become a memory, because emptiness can never leave a trace. It cannot leave any footprints. How can emptiness become a past memory? How can you say 'I experienced'? It is always in the now, it is experienc*ing*. It is neither past nor future, it is always an ongoing process. Once you enter you have entered.

Emptiness can never become a memory, because emptiness can never leave a trace. It cannot leave any footprints. How can emptiness become a past memory? How can you say 'I experienced'? It is always in the now, it is experiencing. It is neither past nor future, it is always an ongoing process. Once you enter you have entered.

When all experiences disappear and you are left utterly alone, nothing to see, only emptiness in the hands, no experience at all, then suddenly you realize yourself. Then you turn upon yourself, then you fall into your source. And that is not an experience, it is a realization. That is the difference between the words "experience" and "realization". It is not that you have seen something, experienced something. Now you know who you are.

When all experiences disappear and you are left utterly alone, nothing to see, only emptiness in the hands, no experience at all, then suddenly you realize yourself. Then you turn upon yourself, then you fall into your source. And that is not an experience, it is a realization. That is the difference between the words "experience" and "realization". It is not that you have seen something, experienced something. Now you know who you are.

I call Zen the only living religion because it is not a religion, but only a religiousness. It has no dogma, it does not depend on any founder. It has no past; in fact it has nothing to teach you. It is the strangest thing that has happened in the whole history of mankind – strangest because it enjoys in emptiness, it blossoms in nothingness. It is fulfilled in innocence, in not knowing. It does not discriminate between the mundane and the sacred. For it, all that is, is sacred.

Life is sacred whatever form, whatever shape.

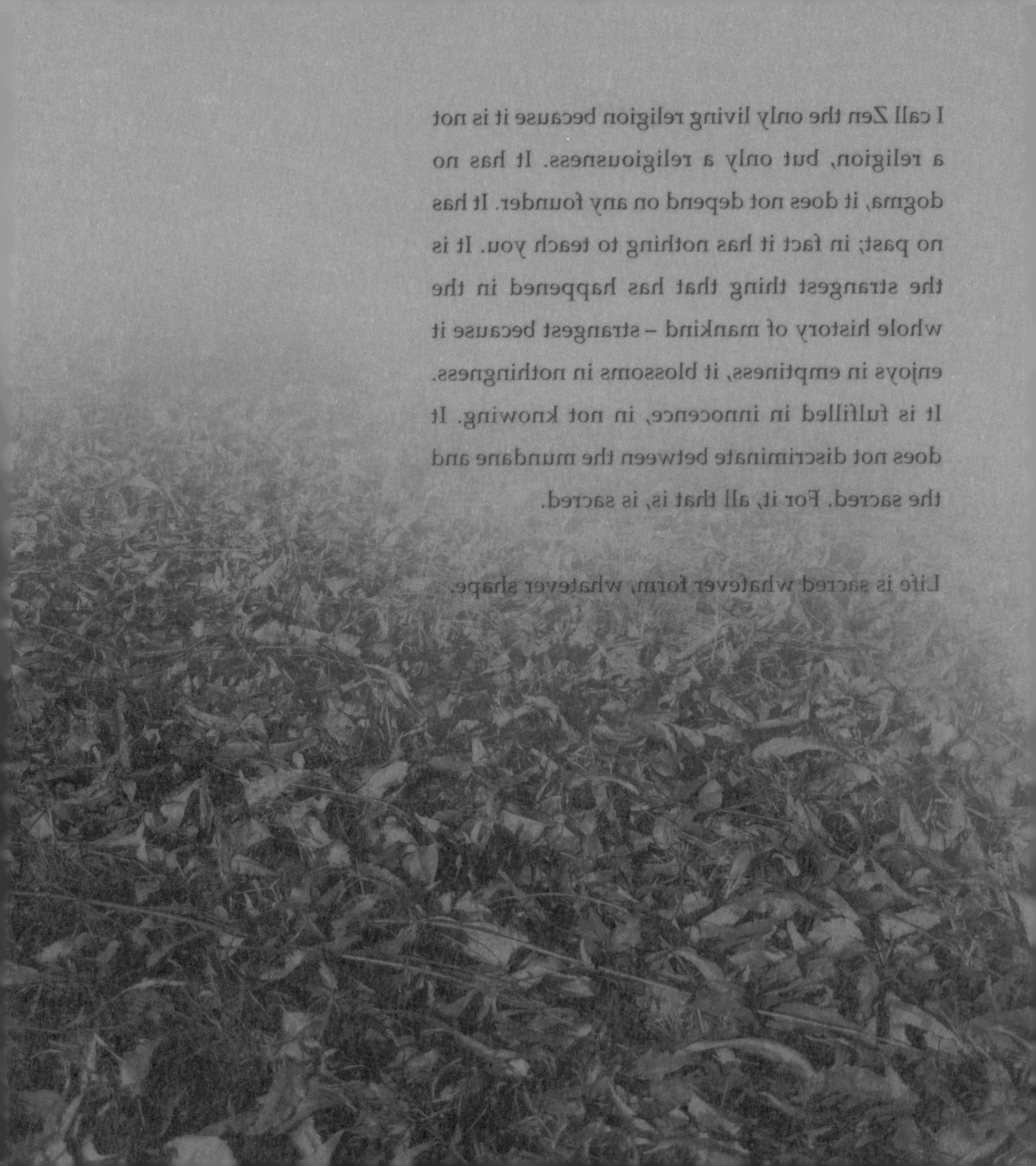

I call Zen the only living religion because it is not a religion, but only a religiousness. It has no dogma, it does not depend on any founder. It has no past; in fact it has nothing to teach you. It is the strangest thing that has happened in the whole history of mankind – strangest because it enjoys in emptiness, it blossoms in nothingness. It is fulfilled in innocence, in not knowing. It does not discriminate between the mundane and the sacred. For it, all that is, is sacred.

Life is sacred whatever form, whatever shape.

Drop the my and you are separate from the mind – that was the bridge. Separate who you are from the mind – just a pure presence, an utter silence, unmoving stillness... and in this space happens all that deep down you are all looking for, knowingly or unknowingly.

Drop the my and you are separate from the mind – that was the bridge. Separate who you are from the mind – just a pure presence, an utter silence, unmoving stillness... and in this space happens all that deep down you are all looking for, knowingly or unknowingly.

Minds are conditioned, always conditioned; they are ready to be conditioned. Minds are bio-computers: they go on absorbing whatsoever is heard. It is a mechanical thing. Put the mind off while listening to me. Be a heart – love, trust. Listen to me in deep emptiness. Don't be there! I am not here – don't you be there. And then something will happen, something will transpire between me and you. Between two nothingnesses the river of truth starts flowing. And it is never conditioning: it is always unconditioning. It will wash your whole being, it will give you a shower; it will cleanse you, purify you.

Minds are conditioned, always conditioned; they are ready to be conditioned. Minds are bio-computers: they go on absorbing whatsoever is heard. It is a mechanical thing. Put the mind off while listening to me. Be a heart – love, trust. Listen to me in deep emptiness. Don't be there! I am not here – don't you be there. And then something will happen, something will transpire between me and you. Between two nothingnesses the river of truth starts flowing. And it is never conditioning: it is always unconditioning. It will wash your whole being, it will give you a shower; it will cleanse you, purify you.

Listen to the gaps, listen to my silence, listen to the silence of the trees and the stars – because silence is nobody's monopoly, it is neither Hindu, nor Mohammedan, nor Christian; it is the only thing which is not monopolized by anybody – and you will start finding the mysteries that I want to speak about.

Listen to the gaps, listen to my silence, listen to the silence of the trees and the stars – because silence is nobody's monopoly, it is neither Hindu, nor Mohammedan, nor Christian; it is the only thing which is not monopolized by anybody – and you will start finding the mysteries that I want to speak about.

Form is emptiness. Man is woman and woman is man, and life is death and death is life. Opposites are not opposites, they are interpenetrating each other, they exist through each other. Form is formlessness, and formlessness is form; the unmanifest becomes manifest, and the manifest again becomes unmanifest. They are not different, they are one. The duality is only apparent. Deep down it is all one.

Form is emptiness. Man is woman and woman is man, and life is death and death is life. Opposites are not opposites, they are interpenetrating each other, they exist through each other. Form is formlessness, and formlessness is form; the unmanifest becomes manifest, and the manifest again becomes unmanifest. They are not different, they are one. The duality is only apparent. Deep down it is all one.

The master is just a device: you can trust the master in deep love, and you can put the ego aside. Otherwise you don't have anything else but the ego – if you put that aside, you will fall into utter emptiness. And you will not be able to fall into that abysmal, bottomless emptiness. You will become very much afraid, you will again cling to anything that you can find around you. And the ego is the closest.

It will be impossible for you to go into nothingness unless somebody is there calling you forth – from your very nothingness, somebody calling you forth, "Come on! Don't be afraid."

The master is just a device: you can trust the master in deep love, and you can put the ego aside. Otherwise you don't have anything else but the ego – if you put that aside, you will fall into utter emptiness. And you will not be able to fall into that abysmal, bottomless emptiness. You will become very much afraid, you will again cling to anything that you can find around you. And the ego is the closest.

It will be impossible for you to go into nothingness unless somebody is there calling you forth – from your very nothingness, somebody calling you forth, "Come on! Don't be afraid."

In the emptiness of truth, where duality ceases, where you cannot even say one is, an unknown phenomenon, which is trust, flowers. Something blooms which is the most beautiful, the most precious, and that is the flower of trust.

In the emptiness of truth, where duality ceases, where you cannot even say one is, an unknown phenomenon, which is trust, flowers. Something blooms which is the most beautiful, the most precious, and that is the flower of trust.

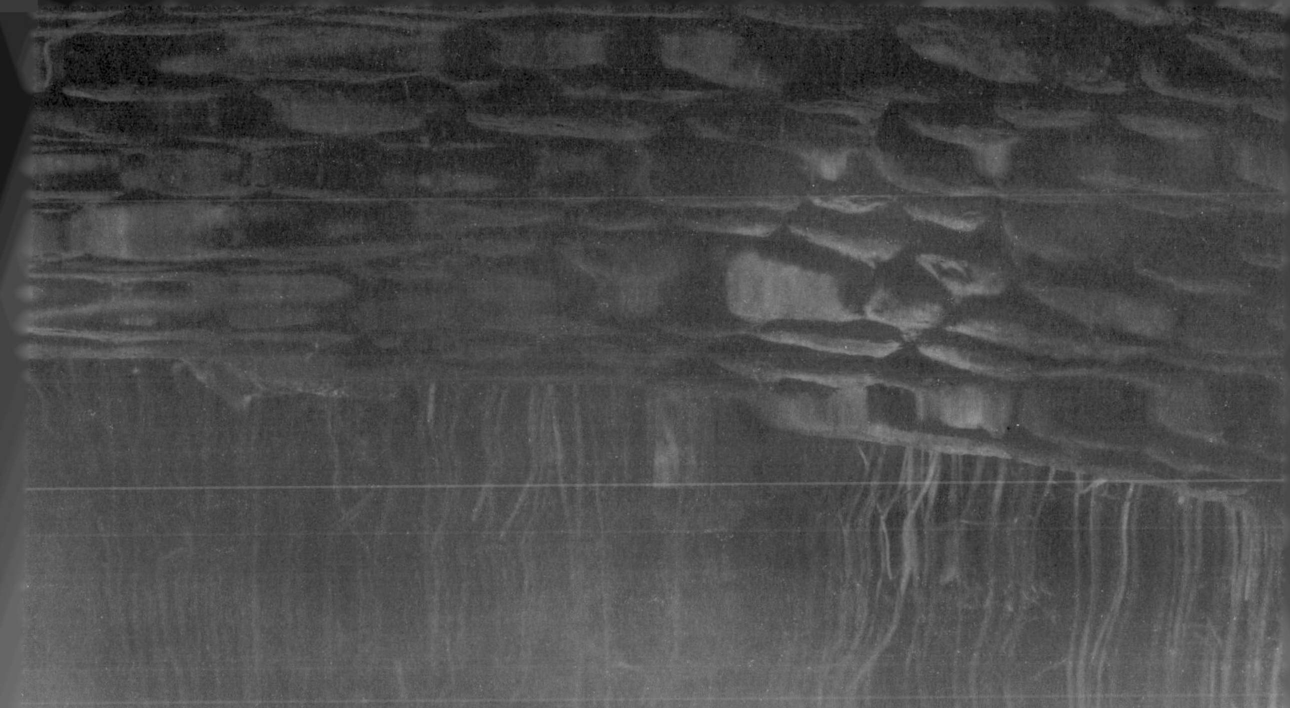

If you will catch hold of the words and you will go astray. Listen to the silence in the words. Words are not important, but the silence that they contain. Listen to the gaps between the words and read between the lines. But to read between the lines you will have to become thoughtless, you will have to become empty. Only an empty heart can read between the lines, because otherwise there is nothing, there is only emptiness. Only emptiness can have a rapport with emptiness.

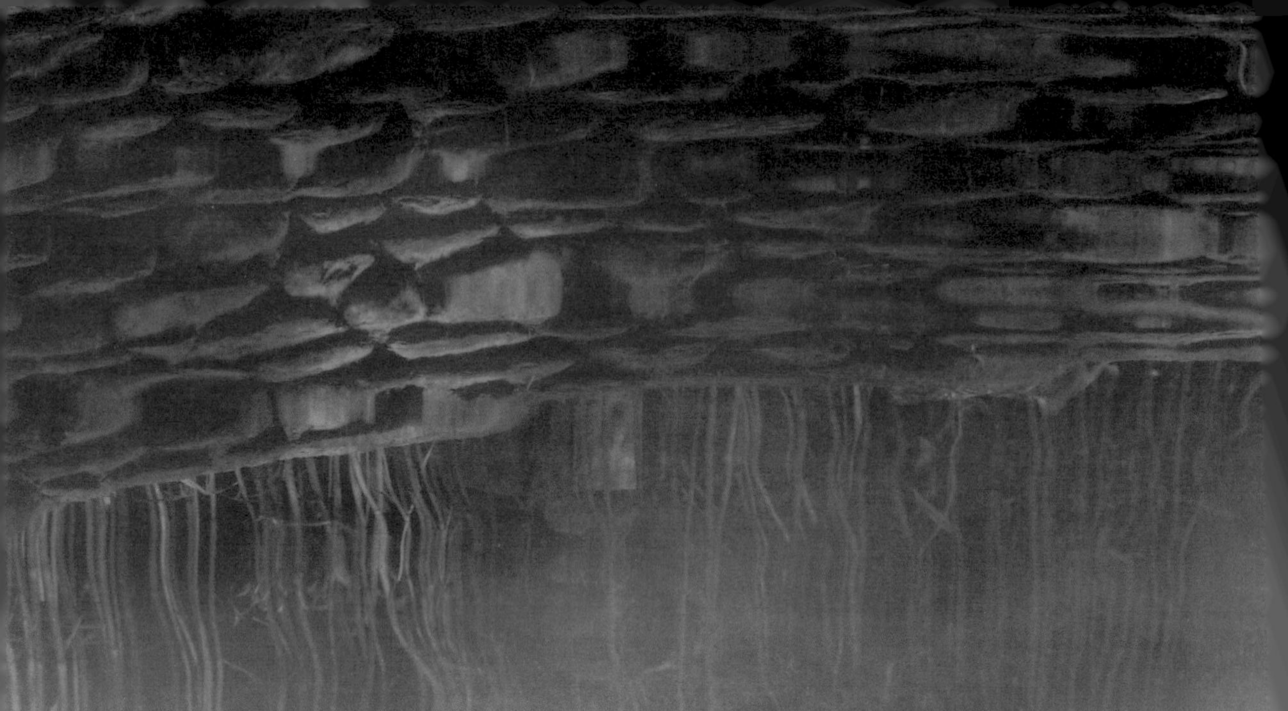

If you will catch hold of the words and you will go astray. Listen to the silence in the words. Words are not important, but the silence that they contain. Listen to the gaps between the words and read between the lines. But to read between the lines you will have to become thoughtless, you will have to become empty. Only an empty heart can read between the lines, because otherwise there is nothing, there is only emptiness. Only emptiness can have a rapport with emptiness.

Shunya is like the sky – pure presence. You cannot touch it although you live in it. You cannot see it although you can never be without it. You exist in it; just as the fish exists in the ocean, you exist in space, in shunya.

Shunya is like the sky – pure presence. You cannot touch it although you live in it. You cannot see it although you can never be without it. You exist in it; just as the fish exists in the ocean, you exist in space, in shunya.

Remember only one thing: your basic nature is absolute silence, serenity, peace, almost a nothingness, an emptiness. And that is your buddha-nature, that is your nature awakened to its own potential. To be aware of it is the greatest experience of life, because it brings liberation from life, birth, death. It takes you out of the wheel that goes on eternally giving you birth and death, and all the agonies and the sufferings. It takes you out into the world of ecstasy, of eternal blissfulness.

Remember only one thing: your basic nature is absolute silence, serenity, peace, almost a nothingness, an emptiness. And that is your buddha-nature, that is your nature awakened to its own potential. To be aware of it is the greatest experience of life, because it brings liberation from life, birth, death. It takes you out of the wheel that goes on eternally giving you birth and death, and all the agonies and the sufferings. It takes you out into the world of ecstasy, of eternal blissfulness.

When I say be totally empty it is coming back to the original source, because through emptiness we are born, and into emptiness we return. Emptiness is the word, really, which is better to use than God, because with God we start feeling there is some person.

Buddha never used "God" he always used *Sunyata* – emptiness, nothingness. In the center you are a nonbeing, nothingness, just a vast space, eternally cool, silent, blissful.

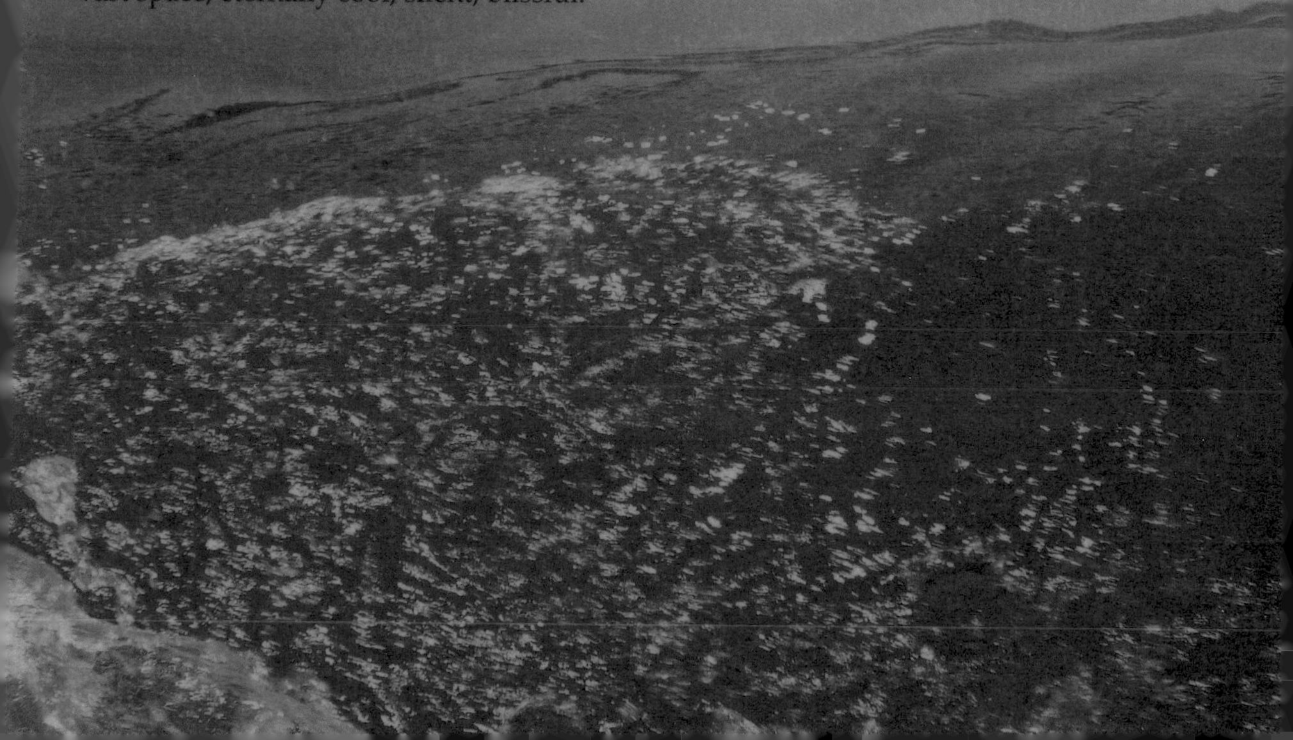

When I say be totally empty it is coming back to the original source, because through emptiness we are born, and into emptiness we return. Emptiness is the word, really, which is better to use than God, because with God we start feeling there is some person.

Buddha never used "God" he always used *Sunyata* – emptiness, nothingness. In the center you are a nonbeing, nothingness, just a vast space, eternally cool, silent, blissful.

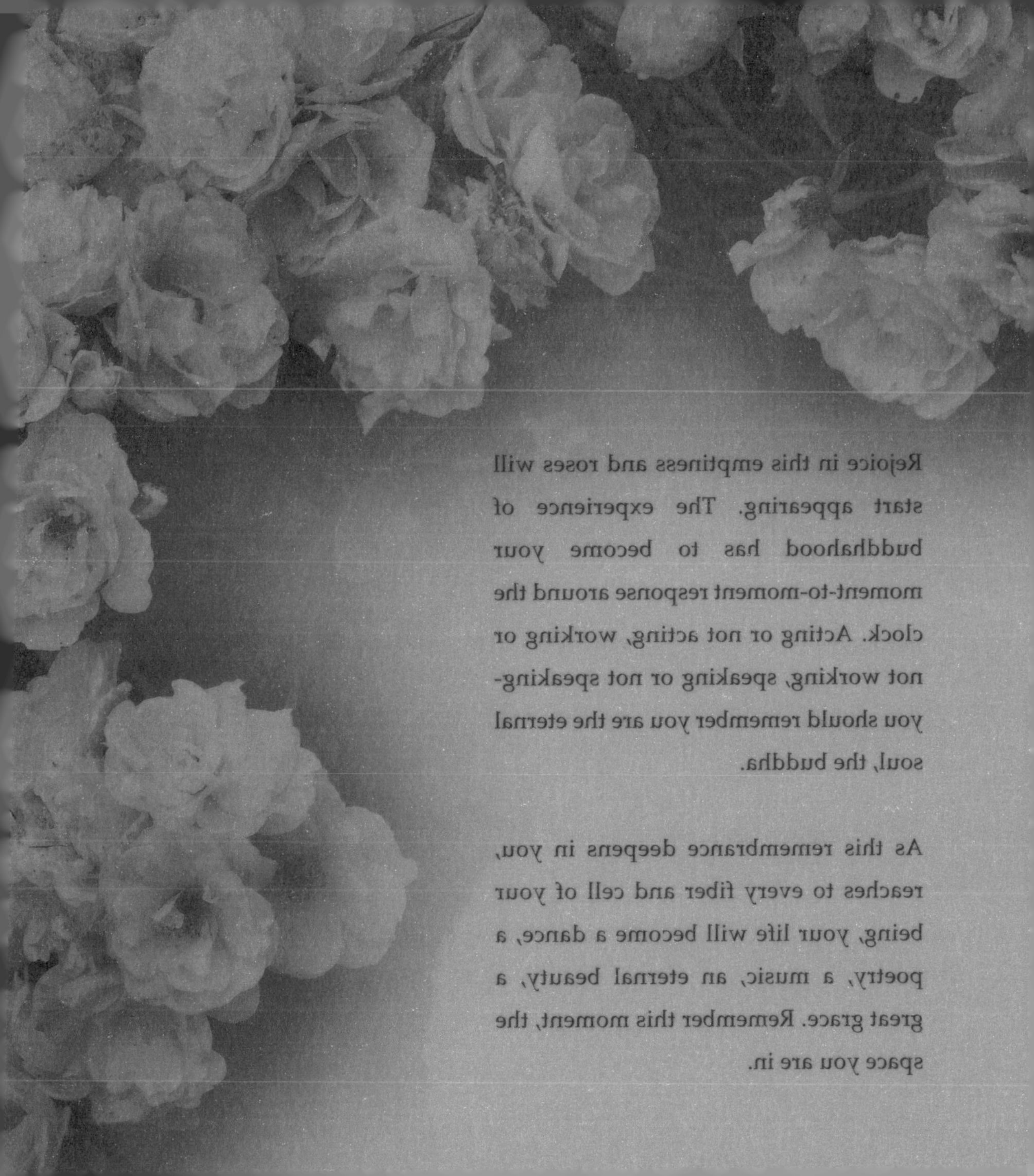

Rejoice in this emptiness and roses will start appearing. The experience of buddhahood has to become your moment-to-moment response around the clock. Acting or not acting, working or not working, speaking or not speaking-you should remember you are the eternal soul, the buddha.

As this remembrance deepens in you, reaches to every fiber and cell of your being, your life will become a dance, a poetry, a music, an eternal beauty, a great grace. Remember this moment, the space you are in.

Rejoice in this emptiness and roses will start appearing. The experience of buddhahood has to become your moment-to-moment response around the clock. Acting or not acting, working or not working, speaking or not speaking-you should remember you are the eternal soul, the buddha.

As this remembrance deepens in you, reaches to every fiber and cell of your being, your life will become a dance, a poetry, a music, an eternal beauty, a great grace. Remember this moment, the space you are in.

When you are not, the whole existence feels ecstatic and celebrates; flowers shower on you. They have not showered yet because you *are*, and they will not shower until you dissolve. When you are empty, no more, when you are a nothingness, *shunyata*, suddenly they start showering. They have showered on Buddha, on Subhuti, on Nansen; they can shower on *you* – they are waiting. They are knocking at the door. They are ready. Just the moment you become empty, they start falling on you.

So remember it: the final liberation is not *your* liberation, the final liberation is *from you*.

When you are not, the whole existence feels ecstatic and celebrates; flowers shower on you. They have not showered yet because you are, and they will not shower until you dissolve. When you are empty, no more, when you are a nothingness, *shunyata*, suddenly they start showering. They have showered on Buddha, on Subhuti, on Nansen; they can shower on you – they are waiting. They are knocking at the door. They are ready. Just the moment you become empty, they start falling on you.

So remember it: the final liberation is not *your* liberation, the final liberation is *from* you.

Beyond enlightenment there is no experience at all, because the experiencer has disappeared. Enlightenment is not only the peak of experience, it is also the finest definition of your being. Beyond it, there is only nothingness; you will not come again to a point which has to be transcended.

Experience, the experiencer, enlightenment -- all have been left behind. You are part of the tremendous nothingness that is infinite. This is the nothingness out of which the whole existence comes, the womb; and this is the nothingness in which all the existence disappears.

Beyond enlightenment there is no experience at all, because the experiencer has disappeared. Enlightenment is not only the peak of experience, it is also the finest definition of your being. Beyond it, there is only nothingness; you will not come again to a point which has to be transcended.

Experience, the experiencer, enlightenment -- all have been left behind. You are part of the tremendous nothingness that is infinite. This is the nothingness out of which the whole existence comes, the womb; and this is the nothingness in which all the existence disappears.